KU-624-997

NATURE WATCH

SHARKS

Michael Bright

Consultant: Ian K. Fergusson CBiol MIBiol

The Shark Trust

HERMES
HOUSE

C O N

This edition is published by Hermes House

Hermes House is an imprint of Anness Publishing Ltd
Hermes House, 88–89 Blackfriars Road, London SE1 8HA
tel. 020 7401 2077; fax 020 7633 9499
www.hermeshouse.com; www.annesspublishing.com

If you like the images in this book and would like to
investigate using them for publishing, promotions or
advertising, please visit our website
www.practicalpictures.com for more information.

© Anness Publishing Ltd 2000, 2006

All rights reserved. No part of this publication may be
reproduced, stored in a retrieval system, or transmitted in
any way or by any means, electronic, mechanical,
photocopying, recording or otherwise, without the prior
written permission of the copyright holder.

A CIP catalogue record for this book is available from the
British Library

Publisher: Joanna Lorenz
Managing Editor, Children's Books: Gilly Cameron Cooper
Senior Editor: Nicole Pearson
Editors: Peter Harrison; Sarah Eason
Designer: Ann Samuel
Picture Researcher: Gwen Campbell
Illustrators: Stuart Carter, Vanessa Card, David Webb
Production Controller: Yolande Denny
Editorial Reader: Joy Wotton

10 9 8 7 6 5 4 3 2 1

The sharks featured in this book are often described
using their common English names first, followed by
their Latin names in *italic*. Where a shark does not have
a common name, only its Latin name is given.

PICTURE CREDITS
b=bottom, t=top, c= centre, l= left, r= right
BBC Natural History Unit: /A James, 25top; /D Hall, 2br,
41cl /J Rotman, 9br, 11tl, 17tl; 17tr; 21tl; 49cl; 57tl; 64t; /M
Dohrn, 44tl; /T Krull, 44br; Bridgeman Art Library: 32br;
45tl; British Museum: 5br; Bruce Coleman/Pacific Stock:
51br; FLPA: /DP Wilson, 25br; 33tr; 51cr; /LS Sorisio, 29bl;
Gallo Images: /G Cliff, 55tr; /J Rotman, 9bl; 10bl; Heather
Angel: 55cr; Innerspace Visions: /A Nachoum, 8bl; /B
Cranston, 5tl; , 17br; , 18bl; , 19bl; 28tl; 29br; 48tl; 57bl; /B
Cropp, 21cl; /B Rasner, 15tr; /D Fleetham, 12tr; 40tl; 50br;
58tl; 63b; /D Flettmann, 1; /D Perrine, 5br; 12bl; 13bl; 14cl;
15tl; 15bl; 16bl; 17cl; 17bl; , 27c; 31bl; 37tl; 38br; 39bl; 40br;
45tr; 49br; 50tl; 54t; 61c; 61bl; 61br; /D Shen, 5tr; 6tl; 62b;
/F Schulke, 57br; /H Hall, 12cr; 32tl; 32bl; /I Rutzky, 49bl;
/J Campbell, 59b; /J Jaskolski, 55cl; /J Knowlton, 50bl;
/J Morrissey, 35br; , 42br; /J Rotman, 31br; , 43bl; 49cr;
59tl; 64b; /JC Carrie, 31cl; /JD Watt, 4bl; 26tr; , 59br; /M
Conlin, 51tl; 53br; 45cr; 53cl; 55tr; /M Snyderman, 10br;
19tl; 19cl; 20br; /M Strickland, 61tl; /MP O'Neill, 54bl;
/MS Nolan, 21bl; 22tl; /N Wu, 54tl; /P Humann, 28bl; /R
Cranston, 11bl; /R Ellis, 49tl; /R Herrmann, 18tr; /R
Kuiter, 2tl; , 6br; 42tl; /R Troll, 48b; 63t; /S Drogin, 20tl; /S
Gonor, 45tl; 58bl; /SH Gruber, 60bl; /T Haight, 25bl; /W
Schubert, 14tl; Mary Evans Picture Library: 55cr; National
Geographic: 60tl; /N Calogianis, 39tl; NHPA: 7cr; 7bl; 24tl;
24bl; /K Schafer, 22bl; /N Wu, 23all; 27bl; , 41tl; 51cl; 59cl;
Oxford Scientific Films: /D Fleetham, 15br; 38cl; 51tr;
57cr; /G Soury, 21br; 26bl; /H Hall, 5tr; 39cr; 46all;
47tl; /K Gowlett, 11tr; /M Deeble&V Stone, 36, 37bl;
/M Gibson, 56bl; /N Wu, 6bl; 62c; /R Herrmann, 20bl; 53tl;
/R Kuiter, 2cr; 42cl; /W Wu, 47tr; 55b; Papilio
Photographic: 16tl; 53bl; Planet Earth: /D Perrine, 56br;
37br; /G Bell, 7l; 10tl; /G Douwma, 22br; /J Seagrim, 33tl;
/J&A Moran, 59cr; /K Amsler, 54b; /K Lucas, 47cl; 52tl;
62tl; /M Snyderman, 5bl; 9tr; 29tl; 47bc; /N Wu, 7tr; 11br;
/P Atkinson, 13tr; Scott Mycock & Rachel Cavanagh: 45cr;
Seitre Bios: 8br; South American Pictures: /R Francis, 45bl;
Universal Pictures: 56tr; Zefa:/M Jozon, 27tl

TENTS

What is a Shark?

There are about 400 different kinds of shark in
the world. Some are as big as whales, others as
small as a cigar. Whatever their size, they all eat
meat. Some sharks eat tiny plants and animals
called plankton. Others hunt down fish, squid,
and even seals. Many sharks will also feed off the
remains of another's meal
or eat animal carcasses.
They live at all depths,
in every ocean, from
tropical waters to cold polar
seas. Some sharks can survive in
the fresh water of rivers and lakes.
Like other fish, sharks take oxygen from
the water as it passes over their gills.
Although some sharks like to live alone,
others survive as part of a group.

▼ CLASSIC SHARK

This blue shark (*Prionace
glauca*) is how most people
imagine sharks. However,
there are many different
families of sharks in the seas
and oceans and with a
variety of body shapes.

no cover over
the gill slits

blue shark's
mouth filled
with sharp
teeth

wing-like pectoral
fins help keep the
shark moving
forward

◄ WHITE DEATH

The awesome great white shark (*Carcharodon
carcharias*) is the largest hunting fish in the
sea. It has an exaggerated reputation as a
killer, partly because a killer shark appears in
the film, *Jaws*. In reality great white sharks
do often eat large prey, but they attack people
only occasionally, in cases of mistaken identity.

► SHARK SCHOOL

Some sharks live alone, others live in schools (groups). Every day schools of female scalloped hammerhead sharks (*Sphyra lewini*) like these gather off the Mexican coast. At night, the sharks separate and hunt alone.

▲ GENTLE GIANT

Although the basking shark (*Cetorhinus maximus*) is the second largest fish after the whale shark, it is not a hunter. It funnels water through its huge mouth, using gill rakers (giant combs) to filter out the tiny plankton that it eats.

triangular dorsal (back) fin for stability

body packed with muscles for strength

flattened tail to help propel (push) through water

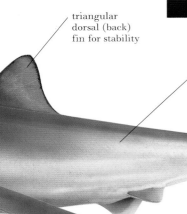

▲ REEF HUNTERS

Whitetip reef sharks (*Triaenodon obesus*) are one of the smaller species (kinds) of shark. They rarely grow over 2m long and hunt along tropical coral reefs at night.

Maya Origins
This monkey head from Central America has been decorated with shark teeth. It is thought that the word shark comes from the Maya people of Central America. It may be based on the Maya word xoc, *(fury). The Maya symbol (word picture) for* xoc *is a shark-like creature.*

Shapes and Sizes

Many hunting sharks have long, rounded shapes, like the slim blue shark and the bulkier bull shark. Angel sharks have a flattened shape suited to hiding on the sea floor, while eel-like frilled sharks swim in the deep sea. Horn sharks have spines on their back, and megamouths (big mouths) have big, blubbery lips! As their names suggest, hammerhead sharks have hammer-shaped heads and sawsharks have elongated, saw-like snouts. Giant sharks, such as the whale shark, are as long as a school bus, and there are midget sharks, such as the Colombian lantern shark, which you could hold in the palm of your hand! Whatever the kind of shark, they are all perfectly adapted for the waters in which they live.

▲ **GROTESQUE SHARK**
The goblin shark (*Mitsukurina owstoni*) has an unusual, horn-shaped snout. This shark seems to have also lived in the dinosaur age. A fossil of a similar shark has been found in rocks that were created about 150 million years ago. Today, the goblin shark lives in very deep waters found off continental shelves.

▶ **DEEP SEA NIPPER**
The pygmy shark is one of the smallest sharks in the world. When fully grown, it is no more than 20cm long, making it smaller than a whale shark embryo (baby). It roams the gloomy waters of the Caribbean Sea, hunting in packs.

pygmy shark
(*Europtomicrus bispinatus*)

▲ **STRANGE HEAD**
The amazing heads of the hammerhead, bonnethead and winghead sharks are shaped like the letter T. These sharks use their hammers to detect prey and to aid swimming.

zebra bullhead shark
(*Heterodontus zebra*)

Did you know? The largest shark ever measured was 12.65m long.

▲ ROCK DISGUISE

Unlike many sharks, the spotted wobbegong shark (*Orectolobus maculatus*) has a flattened shape. It is a carpet shark (a family of camouflaged sharks that lie on the seabed), and disguises itself as part of the coral reef. The tassels under its mouth look like seaweed.

▲ SAFETY SPINES

A striped pattern helps the colourful zebra bullhead shark to camouflage itself (blend in) among corals and seaweed. For further protection, at the front of each dorsal fin is a sharp spine. If swallowed, the shark's spines will stick into the throat of any attacker, forcing it eventually to spit out its prickly meal.

▶ UNDERWATER TIGER

A young tiger shark has pale stripes along its body, which fade as it grows older. The powerful tiger shark (*Galeocerdo cuvier*) has a long, rounded shape, typical of hunting sharks. Some can rival great whites in size.

◀ BIG GULP

The whale shark (*Rhincodon typus*) is aptly named. Bigger than any other shark, it is closer in size to the giant whales. It is the largest fish in the sea, can grow to 12m in length and weigh up to 12 tonnes. With its giant mouth and large gill slits, the whale shark, like the basking shark, is a filter feeder.

Light and Strong

Although most fish are bony, the skeleton of a shark is made up almost entirely of cartilage, which is also found in the human nose. It is lighter and more elastic than bone, and it is this that makes the shark skeleton very flexible. This cartilage structure is strong enough to support a shark's huge muscles, and bendy enough to allow it to move with ease. Because sharks' skeleton cartilage and soft body parts decay (rot away) so quickly after they die, it is unusual to find complete shark fossils (preserved bodies) in ancient rocks. Only the hard teeth and spines are fossilized.

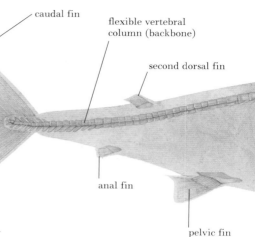

caudal fin

flexible vertebral column (backbone)

second dorsal fin

anal fin

pelvic fin

▼ PROTRUDING JAWS
A shark's jaws are attached to the skull by flexible ligaments. These allow some sharks to thrust their jaws forward when taking a bite.

teeth in upper jaw slice like a knife

▲ DARK TRIANGLE
Like the keel of a yacht, a shark's stiff dorsal fin helps it to balance in the water and stops it from slipping sideways. Most sharks have two dorsal fins, one at the front and one at the back, but some have just one.

▶ AEROPLANE FINS

A shark's pectoral fins, one on each side, act like the wings of an aeroplane. As water passes over them, the fins give lift.

dorsal fin

pectoral fin

gill arches support shark's gills

compact skull protects brain and nasal capsules.

◀ SHARK SKELETON

The skeleton of a great white shark. It is tough, flexible and typical of that found in most sharks, providing support and protection for the entire body. The great white's muscles are attached to a long backbone, the gills are supported by gill arches and a box-like skull protects the brain.

▲ CARTILAGE SOUP

These fins have been cut from sharks and are drying in the sun. The cartilage in a shark's fin helps to make it stiff. When boiled in water it makes a gluey substance that is used in the Far East to make shark's fin soup.

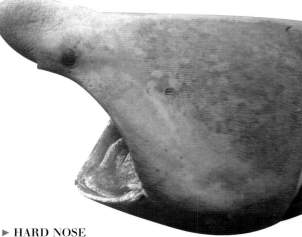

▶ HARD NOSE

The shark pictured above is an adult basking shark. At birth, this shark has a strange, hooked nose, like that of an elephant. When the basking shark starts to grow, the cartilage in its snout gradually straightens.

Tough Teeth

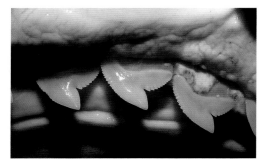

A shark species can be identified by the shape of its teeth alone. Each species has its own distinctive shape, designed for the type of food it eats. Some have sharp, spiky teeth that can hold on to slippery fish and squid. Others have broad, grinding teeth that can crack open shellfish. The teeth of some species of shark change as they get older and hunt different prey. Although sharks lose their teeth regularly, the teeth are always replaced. Behind each row of teeth lie more rows. If a front tooth is dislodged, an extra tooth simply moves forward to take its place!

▲ SHARK SAW MASSACRE

The teeth of a tiger shark are shaped like the letter L. They can saw through skin, muscle and bone, and can even crack open the hard shell of a sea turtle. A tiger shark eats its prey by biting hard and shaking its head from side to side, slicing into its food like a chain saw.

▼ AWESOME JAWS

When it is about to grab its prey, a sandtiger shark opens and extends its awesome jaws. The rows of spiky teeth inside are perfect for grabbing and holding slippery fish and squid. Once caught, the prey is swallowed whole.

sandtiger shark
(Eugomphodus taurus)

▲ NEEDLE POINT

This 2m-long leopard shark (*Triakis semifasciata*) has rows of small, needle-sharp, teeth. Although it is thought to be harmless, in 1955 a leopard shark sunk its tiny teeth into a skin diver in Trinidad Bay, California. This was an unprovoked attack, and the diver escaped.

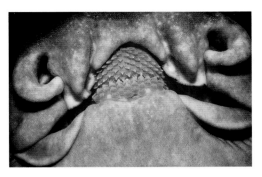

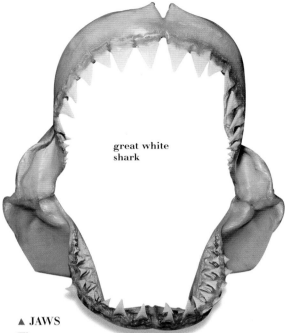

great white shark

▲ JAWS

The awesome
jaws of a great white
shark are filled with two types of teeth. The
upper jaw is lined with large, triangular teeth
that can slice through flesh. The lower jaw
contains long, pointed teeth that are used to
hold and slice prey.

▲ DUAL SETS OF TEETH

The Port Jackson shark (*Heterodontus portusjacksoni*) has small, sharp teeth for catching small fish and broad, crushing teeth that can crack open shellfish.

▼ BIG TEETH

The cookie-cutter is a small shark, reaching only 50cm long. However, for its body size, it has the biggest teeth of any shark known. It uses them to cut round chunks out of its prey, which includes dolphins, whales and large fish.

Shark Man
Ceremonial carvings such as this one were used in ritual dances performed in the South Pacific Solomon Islands. From one dance master to another, these traditional dances were handed down through many generations. They told of myths in which sharks turned into men, and men turned back into sharks again.

cookie-
cutter shark
(*Isistius
brasiliensis*)

11

Never Stop

Sharks are incredible machines, packed with muscle. Some sharks, such as the great white and mako, can even keep their muscles, gut, brain, and eyes warmer than the temperature of the seawater around them. They do this with special blood vessels, which work like a radiator to collect the heat in the blood and send it back into the body. These make muscles more efficient, allowing the sharks to swim faster. They also help these sharks to hunt in seas of different temperatures. Sharks have a huge, oil-filled liver that helps to keep them afloat. However, like an aeroplane, they must also move forwards in order to stay up. Open ocean sharks must swim all the time, not only to stop them from sinking, but also to breathe. Some sharks can take a rest on the seabed by pumping water over their gills to breathe.

▲ GILL BREATHERS
Like this sixgill shark (*Hexanchus griseus*), most sharks breathe by taking oxygen-rich water into their mouths. The oxygen passes into the blood and the water exits the gill slits.

▲ OCEAN RACER
The shortfin mako shark (*Isurus oxyrinchus*) is the fastest shark in the sea. Using special, warm muscles, it can travel at speeds of 35–50 kph and catch fast-swimming swordfish.

◄ SUSPENDED ANIMATION
The sandtiger shark (*Carcharias taurus*) and a few others can hold air in their stomachs. The air acts like a life jacket, helping the shark to hover in the water. Sandtiger sharks stay afloat without moving, lurking among rocks and caves.

► **KEEP MOVING**

Like many hunting sharks, the grey reef shark (*Carcharinhus amblyrynchos*) cannot breathe unless it moves forwards. The forward motion passes oxygen into its gills. If it stops moving, the shark will drown.

swim muscles send ripples down body

spiral valves inside intestines

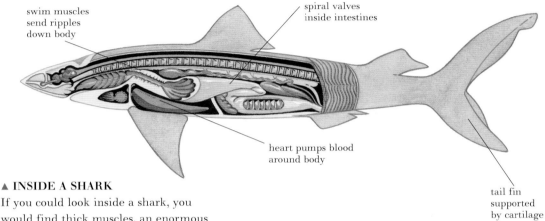

heart pumps blood around body

tail fin supported by cartilage

▲ **INSIDE A SHARK**

If you could look inside a shark, you would find thick muscles, an enormous liver, an intestine with a special, spiral valve, and a complicated system of blood vessels that supply the shark's gills.

Did you know? Mako sharks have been seen to leap 6m clear of the water.

◄ **ABLE TO REST**

The nurse shark (*Ginglymoostoma cirratum*) pumps water over its gills by lifting the floor of its mouth. This allows it to rest on the seabed, yet still breathe. Whitetip reef sharks, lemon sharks, catsharks and nursehounds also do this.

13

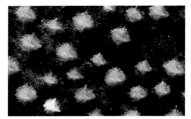

skin teeth of Greenland shark

skin teeth of spiny dogfish

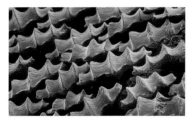

skin teeth of dusky shark

▲ SKIN TEETH
A shark's skin is covered with tiny skin teeth called dermal denticles. These teeth help to speed the shark through the water by controlling the flow of water over its body.

▶ STREAMLINED SHARK
The upper part of the grey reef shark's tail is slightly larger than the lower. Because of this, the tail's downward movement is so powerful that it balances the lift from the pectoral wings. Scientists believe that this helps the shark to move evenly through the water.

Wings in Water

A shark has two pairs of fins (pectoral and pelvic) that work like an aeroplane's wings, lifting the shark as it moves forward. Its dorsal fins and anal fin stop it from rolling sideways, like the tail fin of an aircraft. A shark moves forward in an S shape by rippling a series of waves down its entire body. These waves increase in size as they reach the shark's tail, helping it to propel the body forwards. The shape of the tail can vary from shark to shark, depending on the area of water it inhabits. Sharks that live at the bottom of the sea, such as the nurse shark, tend to have large, flat tails. Sharks that swim in open oceans, such as the tiger shark, usually have slimmer, more curved tails. Both types have a larger upper part to their tail. Sharks that stalk and dash to catch their prey, such as the great white and mako shark, have crescent-shaped tails with top and bottom parts the same size.

▲ SEABED SWIMMERS
Hammerhead sharks have unusually small pectoral fins, which allow them to swim and feed close to the seabed. The wings of the hammer-shaped head give the shark extra lift in the water and allow it to turn very tightly. Hammerhead sharks are very adaptable and skilful hunters.

▲ DEEP SEA GIANT
The megamouth shark (*Megachasma pelagios*) was only discovered in 1976. It lives in deep water and swims very slowly. Megamouth does not chase anything. It eats deep-sea shrimps filtered through its gills.

▲ OCEAN TRAVELLER
The blue shark (*Prionace glauca*) has long pectoral fins that help it to sail through the sea like a glider plane, making long journeys easy. It swims to the surface, then glides effortlessly to the depths before swimming back to the surface again.

▲ OCEAN CRUISER
The oceanic whitetip shark (*Carcharhinus longimanus*) swims in the open oceans and is often present at the scene of sea disasters. It is a very distinctive shark, and can be easily recognized by its dorsal and pectoral fins, which are shaped like rounded garden spades.

15

Brain and Senses

A shark's brain is small for its size, but its senses are highly developed. Sharks see well, and see in colour. They can also recognize shapes. Just as amazing are a different range of senses that allow sharks to pick up sounds and vibrations from miles around. They can detect changes in the ocean currents, recognize smells and follow the trail of an odour right back to its source. Some species have shiny plates at the backs of their eyes that collect light to help them see as they dive to deep, dark water. They also have membranes of dark colour that they draw across the shiny plates to avoid being dazzled by the light when they return to the surface. Sharks even have special nerves in their noses that can detect minute electrical fields, such as those produced by the muscles of their prey.

▲ **ELECTRICAL SENSE**
Like all sharks, sandtiger sharks have tiny pits in their snouts, known as the ampullae of Lorenzini. Inside these pits are special nerves. These help the shark to find food by detecting minute electrical fields in the muscles of its prey.

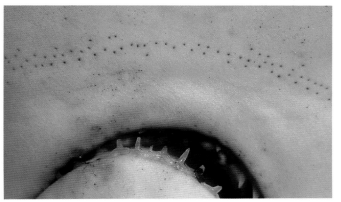

◄ **PREY DETECTOR**
In a hammerhead shark the special pits that can sense electrical fields in its prey are spread across the hammer of the shark's head, helping it to scan for prey across a wide area. The hammerhead searches for food by sweeping its head from side to side, rather as if using a metal detector. It can find any prey buried in the sand below.

◄ SIGHT, SMELL AND SOUND

The nostrils of the hammerhead shark are positioned wide apart on its head. This gives the shark 'stereo smelling' with which it can more easily track odours to their source. But, because its eyes are at the ends of its hammer, it must turn its head from side to side in order to see forwards.

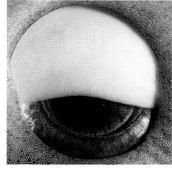

scalloped hammerhead shark (*Sphyrna lewini*)

▲ EYE PROTECTION

When a shark bites, its eyes can easily be injured by the victim's teeth, spines or claws. To prevent this, sharks such as this tiger shark have a special membrane (sheath) that slides down across the eye during the attack.

eye of blacktip reef shark (*Carcharhinus melanopterus*)

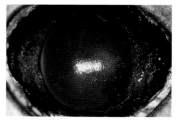

eye of bluntnose sixgill shark (*Hexanchus griseus*)

◄ DEEP AND SHALLOW

The blacktip reef shark has a small eye with a narrow, vertical slit. This type of eye is often found in shallow-water sharks. Sharks that swim in deeper waters, such as the sixgill shark, tend to have large, round pupils.

Did you know? Sharks find their way through mazes as fast as rabbits.

Shark Callers

On the islands of the south-west Pacific, sharks are the islanders' gods. To test their manhood, young shark callers attract sharks by shaking a coconut rattle under the water. Sensing the vibrations, a shark will swim close to the canoe. It is then wrestled into the boat, and its meat divided among the villagers as a gift from the gods.

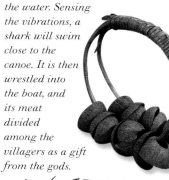

Focus on the Blue

The blue shark is an open ocean hunter. Continually looking for food, it can pick up the sounds and vibrations of a struggling fish from over a kilometre away. From half a kilometre, it can smell blood and other body fluids in the water. As it gets closer, the shark can sense changes in the water that help it locate moving prey. Finally, vision takes over. First, only movements are seen, but then the prey itself. As the blue shark closes in for the kill, it pulls down its eye protectors and swims blind. Its electrical sensors then lead it to its prey.

2 Smells, sounds, vibrations, and water movements attract the blue shark. The movements made by a school of jack mackerel will initially lead the shark to them. It then uses its sight to find an easy target.

1 When hunting, the blue shark uses all its senses to search constantly the ocean ahead for prey. It will also watch the behaviour of other blue sharks in the water, sometimes joining them to hunt in packs.

Shark Hunt

3 Sharp eyesight, quick reactions and an ability to speed through the water all help the blue shark to chase its chosen target. In an attempt to escape, this group of mackerel fish will dart all over the place, then crowd close together to confuse the pursuing shark.

4 As the blue shark closes in to grab its target, a protective membrane covers each eye. At this stage the shark is swimming blind and relies on the electrical sensors in its snout to guide it to its prey. These home in on the electrical field made by the fish's muscles, leading the shark for the last few centimetres.

5 As the shark bites, it extends its jaws and impales its prey on the teeth of the lower jaw. Next, the upper jaw teeth come into action, clamping down on the fish. The shark then removes its lower jaw teeth from the prey, and pushes them forward to pull the fish back into its mouth. The prey is then swallowed by the shark.

Feeding

Sharks catch a variety of foods, eating whatever they can find in their area. Most sharks eat bony fish and squid, but they can be cannibalistic (eat each other). They often feed on other smaller sharks, sometimes even on their own species. Some sharks prefer particular kinds of food. Hammerheads like sting rays, while tiger sharks will crunch a sea turtle's shell for the meat inside. Shortfin mako sharks hunt bluefish and swordfish. Great white sharks eat fish, but as they get older will also hunt seals and sea lions. Sharks will scavenge (feed on dead animals) whenever they can. The bodies of dead whales are food for many sharks that swim in open waters, including tigers, blues and oceanic whitetips.

▲ FEEDING FRENZY
Large quantities of food will excite grey reef sharks, sending them into a feeding frenzy. When divers hand out food, the sharks will circle with interest, until one darts forward for the first bite. Other sharks quickly follow, grabbing at the food until they seem out of control.

▲ FOREVER EATING
A large shoal of mating squid will send blue sharks into a frenzy. The sharks feed until full, then empty their stomachs to start again!

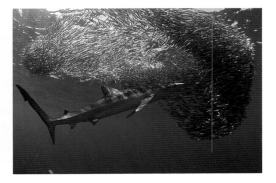

▲ FISH BALL
A group of sharks will often herd shoals of fish into a tight ball. The sharks will then pick off fish from the outside of the ball, one by one.

▶ BITE A BROTHER

Sharks do not look after their relatives! Big sharks will often eat smaller sharks, and sharks that swim side-by-side in the same school will often take a nip out of each other. The remains caught on a fishing line of this blacktip shark show that it has been eaten by a large bull shark.

Did you know? The great white shark sometimes eats crabs and lobsters.

◀ OCEAN DUSTBIN

Tiger sharks are well known as the sharks that will eat not just living things such as fish, other sharks, or dead animals floating in the sea. Tiger sharks have been known to eat coal, rubber tyres and clothes. They are found all over the world and grow to a length of 5.5m. Not surprisingly, tiger sharks have been known to try eating humans.

▼ BITE-SIZE CHUNKS

The cookie-cutter shark feeds by cutting chunks out of whales and dolphins, such as this spinner dolphin. The shark uses its mouth like a clamp, attaching itself to its victim. It then bites with its razor-sharp teeth and swivels to twist off a circle of flesh.

spinner dolphin
(Stenella longirostris)

▲ OPPORTUNISTS

Sharks will often follow fishing boats, looking for a free meal. This silvertip shark is eating pieces of tuna fish that have been thrown overboard.

21

Focus on

1 Huge groups of albatrosses nest on the ground close to the shore of Hawaiian islands, including the island of Laysan. The birds in each group breed, nest, and hatch their babies at the same time. When it is time, the young birds all take their first flight within days of each other.

Sharks can be found wherever there is food in or near the sea. Tiger sharks are rarely seen around some Hawaiian islands in the Pacific Ocean until the islands' young seabirds start to fly. Then the sharks arrive. Any birds that fall into the sea are quickly eaten. The waters are too shallow for the sharks to attack from behind and below as most sharks do. Instead, the sharks leap clear of the surface then drag the birds underwater to drown and eat them. Sharks arrive for their island feast at the same time each year. How they remember to do so is yet to be explained.

2 When ready to fly, a baby bird practises by flapping its wings in the face of the islands' fierce winds. Eventually, the baby must make its first real flight over the ocean. When it does so, the tiger sharks are waiting in the water below.

3 Tiger sharks patrol the clear, shallow waters close to the albatross nests. Their dark shapes can be seen clearly against the sandy sea floor. Every now and again, a tiger shark's triangular dorsal fin and the tip of its tail can be seen breaking the water's surface.

Tiger Sharks

4 Any baby bird that dips into the sea is prey for the waiting tiger shark. At first, the shark tries its usual attack, from below and behind. However, in the shallow waters the shark cannot make a full attack. Rather than hitting its prey at force, the shark just pushes the bird away on the wave made by its snout.

5 After failing to catch a meal, the shark soon realizes its mistake and tries another approach. Its next style of attack is to shoot across the surface of the water, slamming into its target with its mouth wide open. This technique seems to be more successful, and the shark usually catches the bird.

6 The shark then attempts to drag the bird below the surface, to drown it. If a bird is pushed ahead on the shark's bow wave, it will bravely peck at its attacker's broad snout and, sometimes, may even escape. Some birds also manage to wriggle free as the shark grapples with them underwater.

7 Many albatross babies do not manage to escape a shark attack. They are grabbed by the sharks and drowned. Inside the tiger shark's jaws are rows of sharp teeth that can slice into a bird's body like a saw. Sometimes the tiger shark tears off the bird's wings and leaves them aside to eat the body whole.

Filter Feeders

▲ FOOD CHAIN
Eggs and sperm released on the same night by the corals of the Ningaloo Reef in Australia are eaten by the larvae (young) of crabs and lobsters. The larvae are eaten by fish and krill. The fish and krill in turn become food for the hungry whale sharks that swim off the coral reefs.

Some of the biggest fish in the sea eat some of the smallest living things there. Giant species, like the whale shark and basking shark, use their gill rakers to comb plankton (tiny animals and plants) from the water. In the same way as hunting sharks, they use their sharp senses to track down huge areas of food. Whale sharks are often seen near coral reefs, where, at certain times of the year, large amounts of animal plankton can be found. Basking sharks often swim in the area between ocean currents, feeding on plankton that gathers on the boundary. Whale and basking sharks swim in the upper layers of the sea. The giant megamouth shark lives deeper down, sieving out the shrimps that live in the middle layers of the ocean.

◄ WHALE OF A FEAST
Exactly two weeks after the coral has spawned at Ningaloo, the whale sharks appear. By this time, each creature, from the smallest larvae to the reef's fish and krill, will have fed upon the coral's rich food. Each night, the whale sharks swim with their huge mouths wide open, scooping up food which they sieve from the sea's surface.

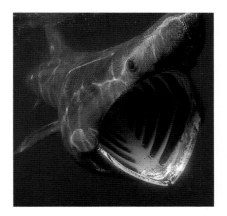

▲ BIG GULP

The basking shark swims slowly through the sea, funnelling food-filled water into its great mouth. In one hour, it can filter 7,000 litres of seawater! When enough food has been trapped, the shark closes its mouth and swallows with one gulp.

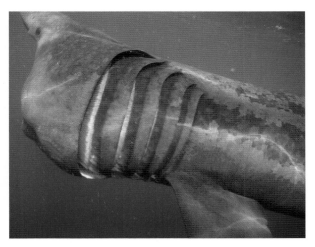

▲ COLD WATER SKIMMERS

The basking shark has gill slits that almost encircle its gigantic body. These are used to filter food, such as shellfish larvae and fish eggs, from the water. The shark passes water through its gill chamber, where enormous gill rakers comb the food from the water.

▲ BIG MOUTH

Patrolling the middle waters of the deep, the megamouth shark scoops up tiny shrimps as they cross its path. Since this shark's discovery in 1976, a further 13 examples have been discovered and some of these have been examined by scientists.

▲ PLANKTON

Plankton is made up of tiny plants and animals that float together in huge clouds on and just below the sea's surface. Both animal and plant plankton are eaten by the basking shark.

25

Keep in Line

No shark is alone for long. Sooner or later, one shark will come across another, including those of its own kind. In order to reduce the risk of fights and injury, sharks talk to each other, not with sound, but with body language. Sharks have a clear pecking order. The bigger the shark, the more important it is. Not surprisingly, small sharks tend to keep out of the way of larger ones. Many species use a sign that tells others to keep their distance. They arch their back, point their pectoral fins down and swim stiffly. If this doesn't work, the offending shark will be put in its place with a swift bite to the sides or head. Bite marks along its gill slits can be a sign that a shark has stepped out of line and been told firmly to watch out.

▲ GREAT WHITE CHUMS

Great white sharks were once thought to travel alone, but it is now known that some journey in pairs or small groups. Some sharks that have been identified by scientists will appear repeatedly at favourite sites, such as California's Farallon Islands, 42km off the coast of San Francisco. There they lie in wait for seals.

Did you know? Some great whites return to the same spot every year.

◄ BED FELLOWS

Sharks, like these whitetip reef sharks, will snooze alongside each other on the seabed. They search for a safe place to rest below overhanging rocks and coral, where, as fights rarely break out, they seem to tolerate each other. The sharks remain here until dusk, when they separate to hunt.

◄ PECKING ORDER

This grey reef shark has swum too close to another, larger shark and has been bitten on its gill slits as a punishment. The marks on its skin show that its attacker raked the teeth of its lower jaw across the sensitive skin of the grey reef's gill slits. A shark's injuries heal rapidly, so this unfortunate victim will recover quickly from its wounds.

► REEF SHARK GANGS

Sharks have their own personal space. As they patrol the edge of a reef, schools of blacktip reef sharks will tell others that they are too close by moving their jaw or opening their mouth. During feeding, order sometimes breaks down and a shark might be injured in the frenzy.

◄ SHARK SCHOOL

Every day schools of scalloped hammerhead sharks gather close to underwater mountains in the Pacific Ocean. They do not feed, even though they come across shoals of fish that would normally be food. Instead, they swim repeatedly up and down, as though taking a rest.

Focus on

By day scalloped hammerhead sharks swim in large schools around underwater volcanoes in the Pacific, the Gulf of California off Mexico, and off the Coco and Galapagos islands. This species of shark cannot stop swimming or it will drown. Schools are a safe resting place for them. Even sharks have enemies, such as other sharks and killer whales, so there is safety in numbers. In schools, scalloped hammerheads can also find a mate. At night, they separate to hunt. They swim to favourite feeding sites, using their electric sensors to follow magnetic highways made by lava on the seabed.

BAD-TEMPERED SHARKS

The larger a female hammerhead becomes, the less likely she is to get on with her neighbours! Older and larger hammerhead sharks like more space than smaller, younger sharks. In hammerhead schools, the relationship between sharks seems to be controlled by constant displays of threat and small fights.

FEMALES ONLY

The sharks in this huge school of hammerheads are mainly females. Larger sharks swim in the centre, and smaller sharks on the outside. Large sharks dominate the group, choosing the best positions in which to swim. Not only is the middle safer, but it is also the place where male sharks look for a mate.

Hammerheads

READY FOR A SCRUB
At some gathering sites, such as Cocos Island in the eastern Pacific, sharks drop out of the school and swoop down to cleaning stations close to the reef. From the reef, butterfly fish dart out to eat the dead skin and irritating parasites that cling to the outside of the shark's body.

BODY LANGUAGE
Larger sharks within a school perform strange movements and dances to keep smaller sharks in their place. At the end of the movement, a large shark may nip a smaller one on the back of the head!

STRANGE HEAD
The scalloped hammerhead is so named because of the groove at the front of its head, which gives it a scalloped (scooped out) appearance. The black tips on the underside of its pectoral fins are another way of identifying this particular shark.

29

Courtship and Mating

Male sharks find female sharks by their smell. The female gives off odours that drift in the currents of the sea, attracting every male shark within smelling distance. The males follow her closely, until one grabs hold of a pectoral fin with his mouth and hangs on tightly in preparation for mating. Fortunately, the female has thickened skin on her pectoral fins, which prevents her from being hurt. The male has a pair of claspers (sex organs) one of which he places inside the female's sexual opening. During mating, the male shark shakes occasionally, to make sure that the female accepts his presence. Once he is sure of this, the male will complete his mating with her.

▲ **ENGAGEMENT IN THE SHALLOWS**
A group of male whitetip sharks will be stimulated by the sexual smell of a female ready to mate. Following her in the shallow waters of a coral reef, the males compete for the female. Eventually, one will win possession by grabbing hold of one of her pectoral fins.

◄ **HANGING AROUND**
Sandtiger sharks hover in the water at special meeting places, waiting for members of the opposite sex. At these sites, lots of shark teeth are found on the sea floor. It is believed that they fall out during the rough and tumble of courtship and mating.

◄ THREE IS A CROWD

Male sharks are usually smaller than females of the same age. Here two males have each seized a female's pectoral fin, but only one male will be able to mate with her.

Did you know? Only one in ten of nurse shark matings are successful.

► NURSE SHARK NUPTIALS

Nurse sharks (*Gingly-mostoma cirratum*) travel to traditional mating sites. The male nurse shark grips the female's pectoral fin and arches his body alongside hers. He will then insert his right or left clasper, depending on which pectoral fin he has seized.

▲ MALE SEX ORGANS

The claspers (sex organs) of male sharks are pelvic fins that have been adapted for mating. Similar to the penises of mammals, they are used to transfer sperm from the male into the female.

▲ MATING SCARS

The courtship and mating of sharks can be a rough affair. Female sharks, like this tiger shark, can be scarred with bite marks made by her mate. However, females have thicker skin than males, which prevents further damage.

Inside and Outside

▲ EGG WITH A TWIST
The horn shark (*Heterodontus francisci*) egg case has a spiral-shaped ridge. The mother shark uses her mouth like a screw-driver to twist the case round into the gaps in rocks.

Sharks bring their young into the world in two ways. Most sharks grow their eggs inside the mother's body, and give birth to breathing young called pups. Others lay eggs in which the pup grows outside of the mother's body. Catsharks and nursehound sharks grow their young in cases called mermaid's purses, which they lay outside their bodies. These can sometimes be found washed up on beaches after a storm. Each mating season, catsharks lay up to 20 mermaid's purses. Inside each is one pup. When the case has been laid in the sea, the mother shark does not guard or look after it in any way. Instead, she relies on the tough, leathery case to protect the pup inside.

▲ TIME TO LEAVE
When it is ready to leave its egg, the baby horn shark uses special scales on its snout and pectoral fins to cut its way out of the tough egg case. On its dorsal fins are tough spines that protect it from the moment it emerges.

Mermaid's Purses
The mermaid is a mythical undersea creature with a woman's body and a fish's tail. In legends, the mermaid lured men to their death with beautiful songs. Catshark and skate cases that are washed up on beaches look like pouches, and are often called mermaid's purses.

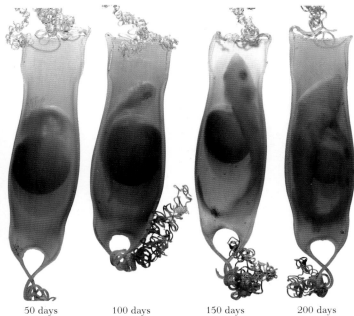

50 days   100 days   150 days   200 days

▲ IN THE SAC

In the earliest stages of development, the catshark pup is tiny. It is attached to a huge, yellow yolk sac from which it takes its food. Inside the egg case, the growing catshark pup makes swimming movements, which keeps the egg fluids and supply of oxygen fresh. After nine months, the pup emerges, with diagonal stripes that eventually turn into spots as it grows.

► SWELL SHARK

The length of time it takes the swell shark (*Cephaloscyllium ventriosum*) pup to grow depends on the temperature of the sea water around it. If warm, it can take just seven months. If cold, it might take ten months. As it emerges, it uses special skin teeth to tear its capsule open.

Into the World

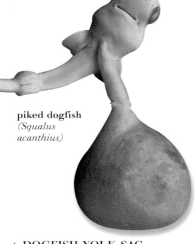

piked dogfish
(*Squalus
acanthius*)

Most sharks give birth to fully
formed, breathing pups. However,
pups grow in many different ways. Baby
nurse and whale sharks start their life in small
capsules. The pups then hatch from the
capsules inside their mother's body, where they
continue to grow before being born. Other
shark pups, like blue sharks, also grow inside
their mothers, in a womb. A sandtiger shark
might have just two pups, but a blue shark can
grow up to 135 at one time. The length of time
it takes a pup to grow also varies. Nurse sharks
take just five months, but frilled sharks take
two years. Some pups feed on unfertilized eggs
inside the womb. Baby sandtiger sharks go one
better. They eat each other.

▲ DOGFISH YOLK SAC
Up to 12 piked dogfish pups can
grow inside one mother. At
first, all the pups are enclosed
in one capsule that breaks after
six months. Each pup then
feeds off its own yolk sac until
it is born three months later.

▶ RESTING
When birth is near,
a pregnant whitetip
reef shark will rest
in a protective area.
This pregnant shark
is resting on rocks
near Cocos Island in
the Pacific. Inside
her womb, she may
develop up to five
pups. Each will be
fed by a placenta
attached to the
womb wall.
The pups are born
after five months.

embryos   womb

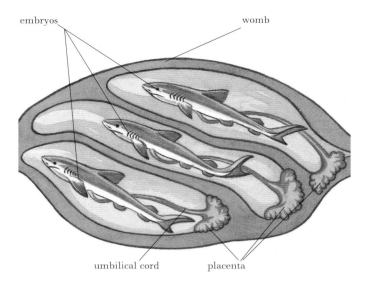

umbilical cord   placenta

▲ WOMB MATES

In some species of shark, such as the whaler shark, embryos develop inside the pregnant female as they do in mammals. At first, each embryo has its own supply of food in a yolk sac, but when this is used up its sac turns into a placenta that attaches itself to the wall of the womb. Nutrients and oxygen pass directly from the mother across the placenta and along the umbilical cord to its own body. Waste products go the other way.

▲ BIG BELLIES

Some baby sharks will eat unfertilized eggs in their mothers' wombs. They eat so much so fast their stomachs become swollen. These baby shortfin mako sharks, caught off the coast of South Africa, have gorged on unfertilized eggs, filling their tiny stomachs.

◀ STRIPED SHARK

Safe inside its mother, this baby tiger shark will have fed on both the nutrients from its yolk sac, and on a fluid produced by the wall of the womb. The pattern of blotches on the newborn baby's skin will form stripes, which will gradually fade as it gets older.

35

Focus on Lemon

A year after mating, pregnant lemon sharks arrive at Bimini Island in the Atlantic Ocean. Here, they give birth to their pups in the island's shallow lagoon where males do not enter. An adult male is quite likely to eat a smaller shark, even one of its own kind. In many species of shark, pregnant female sharks leave the males and swim to safer nursery areas to give birth. Some scientists even believe that females lose their appetite at pupping time, to avoid eating their own young. After birth, however, the lemon shark pups live on their own.

1 By pumping sea water over her gills, a pregnant lemon shark (*Negaprion brevirostris*) can breathe and rest on the seabed at Bimini Island. She gives birth on the sandy lagoon floor to the pups that have developed inside her for a year.

2 Baby lemon sharks are born tail first. There might be 5–17 pups in a mother's litter (family). Each pup is about 60cm long. After her litter is born, a female lemon shark will not be able to mate again straight away. Instead, she will rest for a year.

Shark Birth

3 A female lemon shark can give birth to her pups as she swims slowly through the shallows. The pups are still attached to the umbilical cord when born, but a sharp tug soon releases them. The small remora fish that follow the shark everywhere will feast on the afterbirth.

4 After birth, a baby lemon shark makes for the safety of the mangroves at the edge of the lagoon. Here, it spends the first few years of its life in a strip of mangrove 40m wide and 400m long feeding on small fish, worms and shellfish, taking care to avoid sharks larger than itself. Its home overlaps the territory of other young sharks.

5 To avoid being eaten, young lemon sharks gather with others of the same size. Each group patrols its own section of the lagoon at Bimini. This young lemon shark is about one year old. When it is seven or eight, it will leave the safety of the lagoon and head for the open reefs outside.

Look in any Ocean

Sharks live throughout the world's oceans and seas, and at all depths. Some sharks, like bull sharks, even swim in rivers and lakes. Whale, reef and nurse sharks are all tropical species that prefer warm waters. Temperate-water sharks, such as the mako, horn and basking sharks, live in water that is 10–20°C. Cold-water sharks often live in very deep water. The Portuguese shark, frilled shark, and goblin shark are all cold water sharks. A few species will swim in extremely cold waters, such as the Greenland shark which braves the icy water around the Arctic Circle.

NORTH AMERICA

ATLANTIC OCEAN

PACIFIC OCEAN

SOUTH AMERICA

▶ **SWIMMING POOLS**

This map shows the main parts of the world's seas in which different kinds of sharks live. The key beneath the map shows which sharks live where.

▶ **OCEAN WANDERER**

The oceanic whitetip shark swims the world's deep, open oceans, in tropical and sub-tropical waters. It is also one of the first sharks to appear at shipwrecks.

KEY

whale shark
basking shark
bull shark
tiger shark
white tip shark
Greenland shark
great white shark

◀ **ISLAND LIVING**

The Galapagos shark (*Carcharhinus galapagensis*) swims in the waters of the Galapagos islands, on the Equator. It also swims around tropical islands in the Pacific, Atlantic and Indian oceans.

◄ UNDER THE ICE
The Greenland shark (*Somniosus microcephalus*) is the only shark known to survive under polar ice in the North Atlantic seas. It has a luminous parasite attached to each eye that attracts prey to the area around its mouth.

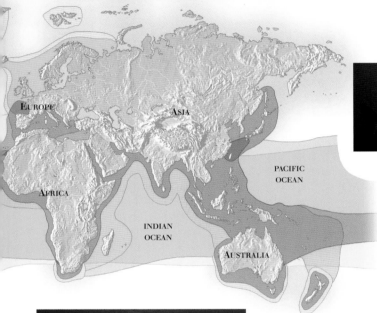

EUROPE
ASIA
PACIFIC OCEAN
AFRICA
INDIAN OCEAN
AUSTRALIA

▲ TEMPERATE PREDATOR
The great white shark lives in temperate, sub-tropical and tropical seas, including the Mediterranean. It usually swims in coastal waters rather than the open sea.

▲ TIGER OF THE SEAS
The tiger shark swims in mainly tropical and warm temperate waters, both in open ocean, and close to shore. Tiger sharks have been seen off Morocco and the Canary Islands.

◄ REEF SHARK
The blacktip reef shark patrols reefs in the Indian and Pacific oceans. It also lives in the Mediterranean and Red Sea, and as far west as the seas off Tunisia, in North Africa.

Upwardly Mobile

Not all sharks travel far afield. Some prefer to stay close to home, swimming only in one small area. Others have a daily routine, spending the day in deep waters, but moving closer to shore to feed at night. A few deep sea sharks make a different daily journey, spending the day in the deep, and rising to the surface to feed at night. Some sharks travel vast distances, crossing oceans. This has only recently been discovered with the tagging of sharks. Rather than killing sharks when they catch them, scientists and fishermen now give them a special tag. Each tag has its own number, which identifies the shark. So, when the shark is caught again, scientists can see how much it has grown, and also how far it has travelled.

sandbar shark (*Carcharinus plumbeus*)

Did you know? A blue shark once travelled a total distance of 7,146 km.

▲ INTO THE GULF

Atlantic sandbar sharks can travel over 3,000km, from the Atlantic coastline of the USA to the coast of Mexico. These amazing sharks grow incredibly slowly, only about 3cm a year. They reach adulthood very late in life, when they are 30 years old.

◄ GIVEN A NAME

This tiger shark has been tagged (marked) by scientists and is being released back into the sea. Tagging has shown that tiger sharks travel great distances across oceans. Previously people had believed that they stayed in one place.

◄ OCEAN MIGRATOR
Female blue sharks in the North Atlantic go on a very long migration. They circle the Atlantic Ocean, mating off North America and then giving birth near Spain and Portugal at the end of their journey.

► EPIC JOURNEY
Female blue sharks travel from North America to Europe where they give birth to their pups. Then they turn back towards the USA. They travel at about 40 km per day. A shark swimming fast might cover the round trip of 15,000km in 15 months.

▼ FOLLOW THE TEMPERATURE
Shortfin mako sharks travel into the North Atlantic, but rarely swim the whole way across. They like to swim in an exact temperature of 17–22°C. They follow thermal water corridors through the ocean to winter in the Sargasso Sea.

shortfin mako shark
(Isurus oxyrinchus)

► DOUBLE BACK
Migrating mako sharks travel to the middle of the Atlantic Ocean and then turn back towards the USA. The sharks do not go further because from the middle of the ocean to Europe the water is not the temperature they prefer to swim in.

41

frilled shark
(Chlamydoselachus anguineus)

The Ocean Depths

Many sharks are rarely seen because they live in the darkness of the deep. Catsharks and dogfish live in these gloomy waters, glowing in the dark with a luminous green-blue or white light. Some of these species travel and hunt in packs, following their prey to the surface at night, returning into the depths by day. Most of the world's smallest sharks live here. Pygmy and dwarf sharks no bigger than a cigar travel up and down the ocean for several kilometres each day. On the deep sea floor are such enormous sharks as the sixgill, sevengill and sleeper sharks. These eat the remains of food that sinks down from the sea's surface. Many deep sea sharks look primitive, but strangest of all are the frilled and horned goblin sharks. These look like the fossilized sharks that swam the seas 150 million years ago.

▲ LIVING FOSSIL

The frilled shark is the only shark shaped like an eel. It has six feathery gill slits, 300 tiny, three-pointed teeth and a large pair of eyes. Instead of a backbone, it has a firm, but flexible, rod of cartilage. These features tell us that the frilled shark resembles sharks that lived in the oceans millions of years ago.

▲ DEEP SEA JOURNEYS

The shortnose spurdog can be recognized by a spine at the front of each dorsal fin. It lives in large packs made up of thousands of sharks. It swims at depths of 800m in the northern waters of the Atlantic and Pacific oceans. Seasonally, the packs make a daily migration, from north to south and from coastal to deeper waters.

shortnose spurdog
(Squalus megalops)

▼ DEEPEST OF THE DEEP

The Portuguese dogfish holds the record for living in the deepest waters. One was caught 2,718m below the sea's surface. At this depth, the water temperature is no higher than a chilly 5–6°C.

Portuguese dogfish
(Centroscymnus coelolepis)

◄ SIXGILL SLITS

Most modern sharks have five gill slits, but primitive sharks, like bluntnose sixgill sharks (*Hexanchus griseus*), have more. These sharks are found at huge depths around the world. They have evolved (developed) slowly, and still have the features of sharks that lived millions of years ago.

▼ SEVENGILL SLITS

Broadnose sevengill sharks have seven gill slits. They have primitive, sharp teeth that look like tiny combs. They use these to slice up ratfish, small sharks and mackerel. Because some of their prey live near the surface, sevengill sharks travel to the sea's surface to hunt at night.

Broadnose sevengill shark
(*Notorynchus cepedianus*)

Did you know? Many deep-sea sharks have light-organs on their bodies.

velvet belly
(*Etmopterus spinax*)

◄ SLIMY COAT

The velvet belly is 66cm long. It lives in the Atlantic and Mediterranean, at depths of 70–2,000m. The velvet belly is covered with luminous slime, and the underside of its body has special organs that give out light. It eats deep-sea fish and shrimps.

43

Freshwater Sharks

Although most sharks live in the salt water of the sea some, such as the bonnethead and sandbar sharks, swim to the mouths of rivers to give birth. There are a few sharks that swim all the way up rivers, and some swim into freshwater lakes. Atlantic sharpnose and spadenose sharks, and Ganges and Borneo river sharks swim in fresh water. Bull sharks are the species most often seen in fresh water. How this species' body copes with fresh water is not known. A fish that usually swims in salt water needs to find a way of coping with water that is not salt. On entering a river or lake, a fish used to salt water would be expected to absorb water and blow up like a balloon, but bull sharks do not. Somehow, they have found a way to keep the levels of salt in their blood low, so reducing water absorption in fresh water.

▲ HOLY RIVER
Shark attacks on pilgrims bathing in the holy Ganges River in India were once blamed on the Ganges river shark. Instead, they were probably made by the bull shark, which feeds on cremated bodies thrown into the river.

◄ RIVER JOURNEYS
Bull sharks have been seen in the Amazon, Congo and Mississippi rivers, and in other tropical rivers and lakes around the world. They gather at the river mouth, where edible rubbish is found during floods. Bull sharks are also sometimes called Zambezi sharks because they make regular journeys up Africa's Zambezi river.

Vishnu

In Hindu religion, the god Vishnu is believed to be the protector of the world. In legendary tales, Vishnu saved the sacred religious texts of India when the whole world was covered in water. This Indian picture shows him emerging from the mouth of a monstrous fish, probably a shark.

▲ KEYS SWIMMER

This bonnethead shark (*Sphyrna tiburo*) lives near river mouths in the Florida Keys, in Florida Bay in the southeast of the USA.

▶ BORN-AGAIN SHARK

The Borneo river shark (*Glyphis*) was believed extinct until one was caught in 1997 by a fisherman in Sabah in South-east Asia. Until then, the only known specimen was 100 years old and displayed in an Austrian museum.

Borneo river shark
(*Glyphis*)

◀ LAKE NICARAGUA

Although they do not live all the time in Lake Nicaragua in Central America, bull sharks (*Carcharhinus leucas*) are also called Nicaragua sharks because they travel between the lake and the Caribbean Sea. It is thought that some female bull sharks swim to the lake in order to give birth to their pups.

Life on the Seabed

People once thought that all sharks died unless they kept swimming. This is not true. Many sharks that live close to the sea floor do so without moving for long periods of time. Wobbegong and angel sharks have flattened bodies that help them to lie close to the sea floor. Their skin colour also blends in with their background, hiding them from their prey as they lie in wait. These sharks take in water through a special spiracle (hole) behind their eye to stop their gills becoming clogged with sand. Some sharks that live on the sea floor, such as catsharks and carpet sharks, are not flattened. Whatever their shape, most are camouflaged with spots, stripes or a mottled pattern on their back.

▲ OCEAN CAMOUFLAGE
Sharks that live near the surface can also camouflage themselves. From above, the great white's dark back blends in with the ocean depths.

▼ SPOTTED ZEBRA
The adult zebra shark (*Stegostoma fasciatum*) has spots instead of zebra stripes. It has stripes on its skin as a pup. These break up into spots as the shark grows. It lives in the Indian and Pacific Oceans.

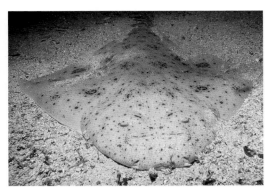

▲ AMBUSH EXPERT

The Pacific angel shark (*Squatina californica*) buries itself in the sand, and watches for prey. When a fish comes close, the shark rises up and engulfs the fish in its huge mouth. It then sinks back to the seabed, swallowing its food whole.

▲ CORAL COPYCAT

This tasselled wobbegong (*Eucrossorhinus dasypogon*) is invisible to its prey. It copies the colour of rock and coral, and has a fringe of tassels hanging down below its mouth that look like seaweed.

► SHELLFISH EATER

The leopard shark lives in the shallow waters of the Pacific, along the west coast of the USA. It swims slowly, searching the sea floor for the molluscs that it eats.

◄ JAGGED SNOUT

The common sawshark (*Pristiophorus cirratus*) has a long snout with tooth-like barbs along each side. Two sensitive barbels (bristles) hang beneath its snout. It mows through sand and seaweed on the seabed, catching its prey by slashing about with its barbed snout.

Prehistoric Seas

The first recognizable sharks lived in the sea 400 million years ago. These early sharks developed from primitive jawless fish. The golden age of the sharks did not take place for another 100 million years. Then, sharks of every shape and size filled the sea and ruled the oceans. They grew into both incredible hunters and giant filter feeders.

About 150 million years ago, all sharks of the golden age began to die out. They were replaced with new breeds of sharks, the ancestors of today's sharks. When the sea-going relatives of the dinosaurs became extinct, sea mammals (warm-blooded animals) began to evolve, and with them eventually arrived a gigantic predator — megalodon. This shark grew to 18m and is thought to be the ancestor of the great white shark. It fed on whales and dolphins, but eventually outgrew its food supply and it died out, too.

▲ CIRCULAR SAW
This strange spiral of fossilized teeth comes from the jaws of a whorl-tooth shark. This creature lived during the golden age of the sharks. Unlike modern species, this shark did not lose its teeth. Instead, they were rotated along its spiral system of teeth, then stored in a special chamber underneath the lower jaw.

whorl-tooth shark
(Helicoprion)

▼ SCISSOR TOOTH
This is an artist's impression of the ancient whorl-tooth shark. This shark had a single row of sharp teeth in its lower jaw, and a scattering of broad, crushing teeth in the upper jaw.

Did you know? Fossil sharks' teeth detected poison.

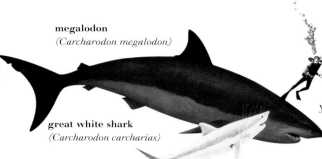

megalodon
(*Carcharodon megalodon*)

great white shark
(*Carcharodon carcharias*)

◀ **MONSTER SHARK**
Today's great white shark might seem a monster, but megalodon was three times bigger. It first appeared about 18 million years ago, disappearing two million years ago. It was the terror of the oceans.

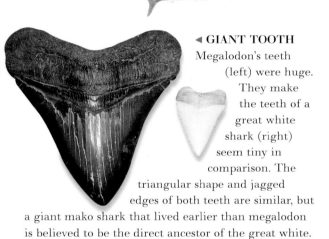

◀ **GIANT TOOTH**
Megalodon's teeth (left) were huge. They make the teeth of a great white shark (right) seem tiny in comparison. The triangular shape and jagged edges of both teeth are similar, but a giant mako shark that lived earlier than megalodon is believed to be the direct ancestor of the great white.

▲ **RECONSTRUCTED JAWS**
Fossilized teeth and some pieces of backbone are the only megalodon remains ever found. However, by using the great white as a model, scientists have been able to reconstruct its huge jaws. Over 2m wide, megalodon's jaws could have eaten several people in one big gulp.

▶ **FOSSIL TEETH**
These fossilized teeth belong to an ancestor of the salmon and porbeagle sharks. It lived about 40 million years ago.

▶ **BIZARRE SHARK**
This artist's impression of the spine-brush shark is based on fossils found in Glasgow. *Stethacanthus* is its scientific name. The shark has a strange spiny brush where its dorsal fin should be. No one knows what it is for.

spine-brush shark
(*Stethacanthus*)

49

Shark Relatives

Sharks have some close relatives. Skates and rays are especially similar to their shark cousins. Both have features that are found in sharks, including a cartilage skeleton, electrical sensors and skin teeth. In fact, skates and rays look like flattened sharks. They also come in all shapes and sizes, ranging from long guitarfish to giant manta rays. Like whale sharks, manta rays also filter plankton from the surface of the sea, but in a more unusual way. Turning somersaults in the water, the rays guide the plankton into their mouths with flattened horns at either side of their head. Another close relative of the shark is the ratfish. Looking like a cross between a shark and a bony fish, the ratfish is probably the long-lost descendant of mollusc-eating sharks that lived 300 million years ago.

▲ STING IN THE TAIL

One of 30 known species of sting ray, the southern sting ray (*Dasyatis americana*) moves through the water by rippling its broad pectoral fins. It uses its tail to dish out a barbed sting to any attacker.

▼ UNDERSEA RATS

Although they are relatives, ratfish look quite different from sharks. In fact, in some ways they resemble rats. They have a long, thin tail, smooth skin and rodent-like teeth. Male ratfish also have an extra, hooked clasper on their forehead, and use two pairs of claspers around their pelvic fins to grip the female.

ratfish
(*Hydrolagus colliei*)

▶ SHARK OR RAY?

The long, flat shovelnose guitarfish looks like a cross between a shark and a ray. Although it uses its tail to swim, it is more closely related to rays. It swims in the coastal waters of the eastern Pacific. An adult usually grows to 1.5m long.

shovelnose guitarfish
(*Rhinobatus productus*)

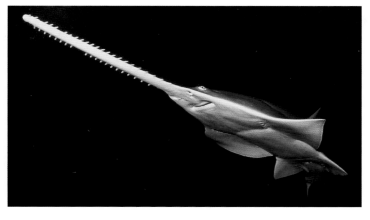

◀ SAW FISH

Saw fish (Pristidae) belong to the ray family. Unlike sawsharks, the pectoral fins of the saw fish grow forwards on its body, and are joined to the side of its head. Its gill openings are found on the underside of its head. It has a broad saw, which is lined with skin teeth that have been especially adapted for hunting.

electric ray
(*Torpedo torpedo*)

◀ ELECTRIC SHOCK

Torpedo, or electric, rays have special blocks of muscle in their wings that can produce electric shocks of up to 220 volts. They use this hidden weapon to knock out their prey. The shock can stun a human.

Did you know? Manta rays may grow to 7m across and weigh 1,400 kg.

▶ FLYING RAYS

Spotted eagle rays (*Aetobatus narinaria*) have broad pectoral fins which they flap like birds. The fins of some species span nearly 3m. Spotted eagle rays feed on shellfish and oysters, which they crush with their teeth.

51

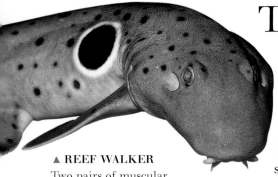

The Eight Families

Sharks fall into eight main orders (groups) divided according to different features. The most primitive order, including frilled and sevengill sharks, have more than five gill slits. Dogfish sharks have long, round bodies, and include luminous (glow in the dark) sharks that live in very deep water. The seven or more species of sawshark have a saw-like snout. Angel sharks look like rays and lie hidden on the seabed. Bullhead sharks have spines on both of their dorsal fins, and carpet sharks, like the wobbegong sharks, have short snouts and bristles on their snouts. Mackerel sharks, with their special, warm muscles, are awesome hunters. These sharks include the great white and mako. The ground sharks include the widest range of all, from catsharks to bull sharks, hammerheads, blue sharks and oceanic whitetips.

▲ **REEF WALKER**

Two pairs of muscular pectoral fins allow the epaulette shark (*Hemiscyllium ocellatum*) to walk over its tropical reef home. It feeds on the seabed of shallow waters around the Australian reefs.

▼ **TYPES OF SHARKS**

Modern sharks are divided into eight large family groups. These groups are divided into over 30 smaller families, and nearly 400 species. This number will probably rise as more species of shark are discovered.

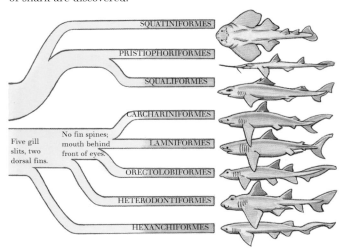

SQUATINIFORMES	Body flattened, raylike. Mouth in front.
PRISTIOPHORIFORMES	Snout elongated and sawlike. Mouth underneath.
SQUALIFORMES	Snout short, not sawlike.
CARCHARINIFORMES	Sliding flap that covers eyes.
LAMNIFORMES	No sliding flap over eyes.
ORECTOLOBIFORMES	Mouth well in front of eyes.
HETERODONTIFORMES	Dorsal fin spines.
HEXANCHIFORMES	Six or seven gill slits. One dorsal fin.

Five gill slits, two dorsal fins.

No fin spines; mouth behind front of eyes.

◀ **PRIMITIVE SHARK**

The broadnose sevengill shark (*Notorynchus cepedianus*) is one of five species of primitive sharks. Each has six or seven gill slits. All swim in deep waters.

▲ **GROUND SHARK**

The swell shark (*Cephaloscyllium ventriosum*) is a ground shark. It blows up like a balloon by swallowing water and storing it in its stomach. When it is threatened, this amazing shark wedges itself firmly inside the cracks between rocks. It can be very difficult to remove.

Did you know? Pacific Island children ride on nurse sharks' backs.

Food for the sharks
The Carib peoples buried the bodies of their dead relatives by ceremonially putting them into Lake Nicaragua in Central America. Many of the bodies were then eaten by bull sharks in the lake. One thief made a fortune by catching the sharks, slitting them open and removing jewels that had decorated the bodies of the dead. Until he was caught, that is ......

▶ **REQUIEM SHARK**

The sandbar, or brown, shark (*Carcharhinus plumbeus*) is a requiem shark, meaning 'ceremony for the dead'. All members of this family are active hunters. They rule tropical seas, hunting fish, squid and sea turtles. They are probably the most modern group of shark.

53

Friends and Enemies

No sharks spend all their time alone. They attract all kinds of hangers-on, including pilot fish, bait fish and a wide range of parasites, both inside their bodies and out! Sandtiger sharks are often seen surrounded by a cloud of baby bait fish. Too small for the shark to eat, the bait fish crowd around it for protection. Basking sharks are sometimes covered with sea lampreys, which clamp on to the shark's skin with their sucker-like mouths. To get rid of these pests, the giant sharks leap clear of the water and crash back down to dislodge them. Smaller parasites live inside each shark. These have adapted so well to life with sharks that they can only survive in one species, some in only one part of the shark's digestive system.

▲ **STRIPED PILOTS**
Tiny pilot fish often ride the bow wave in front of a shark's snout. Young golden trevally fish swim with whale sharks. When they are older and lose their stripes, they leave the shark and return to their reef homes.

▼ **HITCHHIKER**
A remora fish stays with a shark for most of its life. Its dorsal fin is designed like a sucker, which the fish uses to attach itself to the shark's belly. The fish then feeds on scraps from the shark's meal.

▶ SCRAPING CURE

Some fish use the shark's rough, sandpaper-like skin to remove their own parasites. Rainbow runner fish will rub against a whitetip reef shark's side. Behind one shark might be an entire group of fish lining up for a scrub.

◀ BARBER SHOP

Many sharks visit what scientists call cleaning stations. Here, small fish and shrimps remove dead skin and parasites from the shark's body, even entering the gills and mouth. This hammerhead shark is gliding past a cleaning station where several king angel fish have darted out to clean it.

▼ UNWELCOME FRIENDS

Strings of parasitic copepod eggs trail behind the dorsal fin of this shortfin mako shark. These parasites will have little effect on the shark's life, but if large numbers of parasites grow inside the shark, it can die.

▶ BLOOD SUCKER

A marine leech feeds by attaching itself to any part of the shark's skin and sucking its blood. Other parasites feed only on certain areas of the shark's body, like the gills, mouth and nasal openings.

mako shark
(*Isurus oxyrinchus*)

Did you know? Pilot fish ride sharks' bow waves like dolphins on ships.

Sharks and People

Sharks are feared because they attack people. However, only a few such attacks take place each year. People are more likely to be killed on the way to the beach than be killed by a shark in the water. Fortunately, attitudes are changing. Today, people have a healthy respect for sharks, rather than a fear of them. As we come to understand sharks, instead of killing them, people want to learn more about them. Diving with sharks, even such known threats as the great white shark or bull shark, is more accepted. People study sharks either from the safety of a cage or, increasingly, in the open sea without any protection. Such is our fascination with sharks that aquariums are being built all over the world. Here, more people will be able to learn about sharks at first hand, and not even get wet!

Jaws

The book and film Jaws *featured an enormous great white shark that terrorized a seaside town. The film drew great crowds and its story terrified people all over the world. It also harmed the reputation of sharks, encouraging people to see them as monsters, rather than the extraordinarily successful animals that they are.*

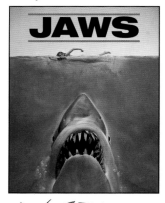

◀ FEEDING TIME

At tourist resorts in the tropics, divers can watch sharks being fed by hand. This activity is not always approved of. Sharks come to rely on this free handout, and may become aggressive if it stops. Inexperienced divers may also not know how to behave with sharks, resulting in accidents, although these are rare.

◀ ANTI-SHARK MEASURES

Anti-shark nets protect many popular South African and Australian beaches. Unfortunately, these nets not only catch sharks, like this tiger shark, but also other sea life, including dolphins and turtles. Less destructive ways of reducing people's fear of attack have yet to be invented.

▶ SHARK POD

Although a similar system is not yet available to bathers, one anti-shark invention seems to work for divers and, possibly, surfers, too. A shark pod can produce an electric field that interferes with the electrical sensors of a shark, encouraging the animal to keep its distance.

◀ SHARK ATTACK

Occasionally, sharks do attack. While diving in Australian waters, Rodney Fox was attacked by a great white shark. Rodney was possibly mistaken for a seal. He is probably alive because he did not have enough blubber on him to interest the shark and he was able to get away.

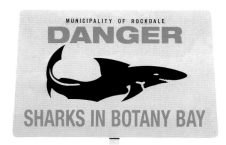

MUNICIPALITY OF ROCKDALE
DANGER
SHARKS IN BOTANY BAY

▲ SHARK WARNING

On many beaches, shark warning signs are used to tell people that sharks might be present. During the day, danger of attack is low, but it increases at night, when the sharks move inshore to feed.

Focus on the Great

The great white shark grows to over 6m long and is the largest hunting fish in the sea. Its powerful jaws can bite a full-grown elephant seal in half. Many people believe that the great white will attack people readily. This is not true. In the whole world, only about ten people a year are bitten by great whites. Great whites are aggressive, powerful fish and will attack people when they mistake them for their natural prey, such as seals. If they realize their mistake, there is a chance that a person can survive — that is, if the blood loss from the first bite can be stopped.

INTELLIGENT SHARK

The great white shows signs of 'intelligent' planning. It stakes out places off the Farallon Islands to the west of San Francisco, USA, where young elephant seals swim. In this way it avoids the large, possibly aggressive, adult bulls that could do it damage.

BODY PERFECT

The great white has the torpedo shape typical of a hunting shark. Its crescent-shaped tail, with its equal upper and lower parts, helps the shark to speed through the water. Although it is called the great white, it is not white all over, but grey on top and white underneath.

White Shark

GIANT SHARK ENCOUNTER

A great white shark dwarfs any diver. To a diver in a cage, it can sometimes seem that a shark is trying to attack. In reality, the shark's electrical sensors are probably confused. The diver's metal cage produces an electrical field in seawater — the shark is then likely to react to the cage as if it were prey.

TERRIBLE JAWS

As a great white rises to take bait, its black eyes roll back into their protective sockets. Its jaws thrust forward, filled with rows of triangular teeth ready to take a bite. This incredible action takes place in little more than a second.

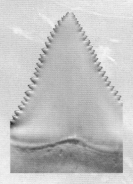

SHARP TEETH

The powerful, arrow-shaped teeth in the upper jaw of a great white have a serrated (jagged) edge. These teeth can slice through flesh, blubber and even bone. The shark saws through the tissue of its prey by shaking its head from side to side.

GAME FISH

To fishermen who hunt great whites for sport, the large breeding female sharks are the most attractive. The killing of these sharks has brought them near extinction in some places.

Conservation

Sharks take a long time to grow to adulthood. They have very few offspring and may breed only every other year. Added to these factors, the hunting and killing of sharks can quickly reduce their numbers. This happened at Achill Island, on the Irish coast, where large numbers of basking sharks quickly disappeared, killed for their oil. Off the coasts of South Australia and South Africa, the great white shark was hunted as a trophy for many years. Numbers of great whites were so reduced that the hunting of them has since been banned internationally. A few countries control the fishing of sharks, to try to conserve (protect) them. However, in other countries, sharks are still hunted for shark fin soup, unusual medicines, and souvenirs. They are also sold to supermarkets as shark steak. Sharks, it seems, have more to fear from people than people have to fear from sharks.

Flying Tigers
A Japanese god of storms is known as the shark man. In ancient Japanese legend, the shark man was terrifying. Encouraged by this fear of the shark, Allied airmen fighting the Japanese during World War II painted a tiger shark on their aircraft as a talisman. The pilots of these planes soon became known as "the flying tigers."

◄ **WASTED SHARKS**
Each summer, many sharks are killed in fishing tournaments off the east coast of the USA. Sports fisherman are now learning to tag sharks, returning them to the sea alive instead of killing them. By tagging sharks, our understanding of shark biology is increased.

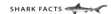

► **CRUEL TRADE**

Caught by fishermen, this whitetip reef shark has had its valuable fins removed. The shark was then thrown back into the sea, still alive. Without its fins, a shark is unable to move and, therefore, feed. It will quickly starve to death. This awful process, called finning, has been banned by some countries.

◄ **TRAVELLING INTO TROUBLE**

This tiger shark is being tagged to track its movements. Shark tagging programmes like this show that many sharks travelling great distances are being netted by several fisheries along their routes. Unless shark fishing is controlled internationally, far-travelling sharks will probably disappear from the sea altogether.

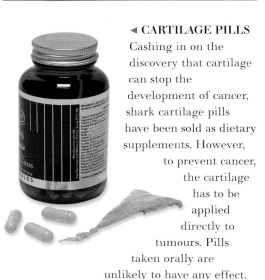

◄ **CARTILAGE PILLS**

Cashing in on the discovery that cartilage can stop the development of cancer, shark cartilage pills have been sold as dietary supplements. However, to prevent cancer, the cartilage has to be applied directly to tumours. Pills taken orally are unlikely to have any effect.

▲ **MULTIMILLION DOLLAR SOUP**

Shark fin soup is made from the dried fins of a shark. It has been prepared by chefs in oriental countries for over 2,000 years. The soup was once served to show favour to an honoured guest, and was also thought to be a health-giving food. Today, it is sold in cans and can be bought in supermarkets.

61

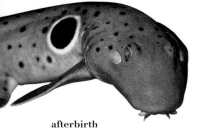

GLOSSARY

afterbirth
Any birth membranes and other tissues discarded or discharged into the sea when a baby shark is born.

bioluminescence
The production of light by living organisms.

camouflage
The way in which an animal blends in with its background or resembles another animal or object.

cannibalism
Animals eating others of their own kind.

cartilage
The strong but flexible material from which the skeletons of sharks and rays are made, rather than the bone that is found in most other animals with backbones.

catshark
The common name given to a group of sharks that are known in the British Isles as dogfish.

clasper
The male sexual organs in sharks, consisting of two modified pelvic fins.

dorsal fin
The tall triangular fin on a shark's back. Some sharks have two dorsal fins, the front fin larger than the back one.

egg case
The leathery covering that protects a shark embryo developing outside its mother's body.

electrical field
A zone of electricity surrounding an object, such as a muscle or nerve cell, that generates electricity, .

embryo
The early stage of an animal before birth.

feeding frenzy
The name for what happens when sharks go berserk, slashing and biting anything that moves, when there is blood in the water or when they are presented with large quantities of food.

filter-feeder
Animals that sieve water through giant combs called gill rakers, for very small particles of food.

fish ball
The ball that schools of fish make when attacked.

gestation
The period of time between conception and the birth of an animal.

gill arch
The part of the skeleton that supports the gills.

gills
The organ used by aquatic animals, such as sharks, for breathing.

gill slit
The vertical openings on either side of the shark, just behind the head, from which the water taken in through the mouth and passed over the gills leaves its body.

gut
The long tube in which food is digested and absorbed, running a winding path through an animal's body.

jawless fish
Primitive fish with sucker-like mouths rather than true jaws. They had their origins 500 million years ago and living descendants include lampreys and hagfish.

krill
Small shrimp-like creatures that swim in huge shoals. Krill form part of the diet of filter feeders such as whale sharks.

ligament
A band of white, fibrous tissue that cannot stretch. It connects bones in a joint and strengthens them.

light organs
Special structures in a fish's skin that produce 'cold' light. They work either by mixing particular chemicals together or with the help of luminous bacteria that do it for them.

megalodon
A gigantic shark ancestor that first appeared 18 million years ago. It is thought to be the ancestor of the great white shark.

nutrients
Chemicals in food that, when digested, build blood, bone and tissue. This tissue maintains growth and strength in the body.

parasite
An organism that lives on or in another living thing (its host), using the host as a source of food and shelter.

pectoral fins
The pair of large wing-like fins on either side of a shark's body.

pelvic fins
The pair of small fins on the underside of a shark's body behind the pectoral fins.

placenta
A disc-shaped organ that is attached to the lining of the womb during pregnancy. It is through this that the embryo receives oxygen and nutrients.

plankton
Tiny aquatic organisms that drift with the water movements in the sea or in lakes.

primitive
Keeping physical characteristics that may have origins millions of years ago.

pup
A young shark, particularly when it has just been born.

pupil
The opening, which can be round or slit-like, through which light passes to the eye of an animal.

receptor
A cell or part of a cell that is designed to respond to a particular stimulus such as light, heat or smell.

remora
A streamlined fish that attaches itself to a shark's body with a sucker, and accompanies its larger companion everywhere.

scavenger
An animal that feeds on animals that have died naturally or were the prey of other predators.

sensory system
The collection of organs and cells by which an animal is able to receive messages from its surroundings.

species
A group of individuals that can breed successfully together. When naming animals scientifically, this is the basic unit of classification.

spiracle
A modified gill slit positioned behind the eye in sharks and rays.

spiral valve
A complicated folding of the tissues in the intestine of sharks that aids efficient digestion of nutrients.

thermal corridor
A layer of water at a particular temperature.

threat display
The aggressive behaviour shown by some species of sharks when confronted by other sharks or sea creatures.

tooth whorl
A spiral arrangement of the teeth in some species of extinct sharks.

vertical migration
The daily movement that sharks make downwards into the deep sea by day and upwards to the surface waters at night.

yolk sac
An outgrowth of the embryo's gut containing food that sustains the shark embryo before it is born. As the yolk is used up the sac is withdrawn into the embryo's body.

INDEX